# Change Your Subconscious and Accomplish:
## Manifesting Affirmations

Shelby Parris

Shelby Parris

ISBN: 9781096856948
ISBN-13: 978-1096856948

This book is filled with affirmations that I consciously used when I realized that the power of affirmations was THE DECLARATION to manifestation. I spoke these words and started consciously manifesting everything I desired into my life. These are the words I spoke when it came to manifesting my success, money, a Porsche, playing professionally, meeting the right people, and being the love I AM.

## Manifesting Affirmations

There is no special or specific way to affirm and manifest. There is no secret that affirmations is the root of manifestation. Again, we are always creating, consciously and subconsciously. Whether you read the original *Change Your Subconscious and Accomplish* then this one or *Unavoidable Truths,* you realized that you have the control over YOUR mind and YOUR life. The irony with rewiring the subconscious mind is that you have to make a conscious effort for it to happen. And consciousness is external. So to rewire the subconscious mind, if you haven't noticed already, takes conscious thinking and action, external, to rewire our subconscious mind to now reflect back things of our true desire, which is proven through the universe again through our thoughts words and actions. In the last few years after realizing the power and studying the *how* when it comes to the subconscious mind I started to manifest so much! If you follow me on Instagram you've witnessed many of my manifest already. All I do is apply *TDA* to everything I desire. I've manifested to be a professional basketball player, grades, food, people, situations, success, cars, clothes, shoes, messages, calls. But realize it is a process to manifesting. And all does not just happen instantly in the 3D world, until you reach that point, but for now much takes *time.* But that time can be seconds, minutes, hours, and not just years, months, weeks.

Now you may not trust in astrology but astrology is based on the universe. The seasons are based on the connection of ONENESS of all. Sky to ground, sun rise in the east to set in the west. The shift of tides and water based on the moon and sun all is connected. I'm not saying that every horoscope post you see is 100% accurate. Yes what it may say for Pisces this day can be the same for Leo this day. Have you ever considered it's because we're all ONE? We're all the same just reflections of different parts and play different roles. New moons and full moons are important for manifesting. Trusting the angel numbers and jumping into TDA when you see them is important. Your angels are around and encouraging you because the universe is on your side. Pronoia.

When manifesting raise your vibrations as high as you feel you can. Ways to raise your vibrations are listed in *Unavoidable Truths*. Again you can affirm anywhere at any time. You do not have to sit in lotus pose or meditation to affirm. Stop the superstition that you have to "Move in silence." No you do not have to announce your moves, but affirmations are to be stated boldly and loud. Yes you can consciously be affirming just within your head, but you give more power to your words when you state them out loud. Again, what you consciously state, external, is heard then internalized by the subconscious. When you think it, say it, then hear it you now aligned and created your affirmation into a trinity. Use THE DECLARATIONS as ways to raise your vibrations and carry out the statements. Affirm as if it already is. Because it already is. Again, all is happening simultaneously. You have it, it has been created. Now you manifest and accept it.

When using THE DECLARATION incorporate all the senses. Visualize what you're affirming, Smell what you're affirming, Hear the sounds of what you're affirming around you, Taste it if you can, go visit and touch what you're affirming; feel yourself already as is! I still go to the dealership and visit and be with my cars. I check up on my Bentley, Lambo, Rolls, and Aston a few times a month. Walk it, speak it, BE it, what you're affirming. Do not over complicate this process. Remember; what is life? Easy.

Few tools I found useful when manifesting:

- Quiet
- Meditating
- Write it down
- Playing Zen music
- Playing a song that refers to my desire's state
- Crystals
- Grounding
- Massage/chiropractic
- Showering while affirming your releases
- Writing down what you're releasing then burning it
- Physically run or exercise and visualize yourself outrunning and leaving what you're releasing in the past
- Sage
- Mudra
- Break something and let your emotions loose
- Water
- Nature
- Be with the object you're manifesting

- Be in the setting you're manifesting
- Cleaning your affirmation space
- Candles
- A picture of your manifest
- Vision/affirmation board
- Vision/affirmation journal
- Affirmation notes to keep on me

Affirm as it's already done. The universe does not know a *right* or *wrong*, *good* or *bad*. The universe is a naïve and anxious secretary that wants nothing but to please you. It takes everything literal. What you declare to it it creates. You are constantly depositing and withdrawing from your karmic debt account. You have two accounts. One for positive and one for negative energy. You are always depositing in both. BE aware that what you state and declare will be withdrawn at one point.

Manifest do not come in the time *we* (self) would like. They come in divine timing. When we are in alignment and truly ready to receive. Some come *faster* because you already vibrate at this level. You have mastered this level consciously and/or subconsciously that it seems to manifest instantly.

When your manifest arrives it's because you earned it. Whether it may be a manifest you like or dislike. If it is less than what you desired than be more specific to the universe. The universe is a naïve secretary. It must be told exactly what to do. Be intentional and deliberate with your affirmations. State the deadline, color, size, etc. of the manifest. Most importantly state the purpose. Just like many kids the universe requires a *why*. Tell the universe why so it fulfills your manifest for the purpose you are using it for.

Give the universe an exchange. You cannot ask for something and give nothing in return. What is your intent? What is your sacrifice? What is your purpose?

When your manifest arrives do not defer it. You proved to father-universe you are capable of handling it. Do not lose or abuse it. Appreciate and grow it. When the manifest first arrives you are tested. Do not be greedy and ask for more. You have enough, use it in the most efficient manner to grow your manifest. The more you water the flower the larger it grows. The more you water your manifest the more father-universe waters you.

THE DECLARATION can be used all the time anytime. Use them when you feel low, use them when you feel high. Use these on a regular basis. Study these mantras. Keep this with you. This is your affirmation bible. Highlight and save ones that are most efficient and applicable for your life. Write and create your own. Continue to affirm confidently, boldly, limitlessly. Life itself is a miracle. You're here to experience. To do that you must create.

# MANIFESTING AFFIRMATIONS

.

**"I AM LOVE**
**I AM PROSPEROUS**
**I AM SUCCESSFUL**
**I AM ABUNDANT"**

**"THE UNIVERSE IS**
**CATCHING UP TO ME"**

**"I DESERVE ALL THAT**
**I MANIFEST"**

**"THAT WHICH I SEEK**
**IS SEEKING ME. I DON'T**
**FOCUS ON HOW IT WILL**
**COME I FOCUS ON MY**
**HEART'S DESIRE. MY**
**HIGHERSELF KNOWS**
**WHAT TO DO TO MAKE IT**
**HAPPEN. I RELAX AND LET**
**GO. ALL THAT IS REQUIRED**
**FOR THE FULLFILLMENT**
**OF MY HEART'S DESIRE IS**
**LOVINGLY AND HARMONIOUSLY**
**DRAWN TO ME. I ACCEPT THIS**
**OR SOMETHING GREATER"**

**"I AM READY RECEPTIVE
AND GRATEFUL
AND SO IT IS. ASE"**

**"MONEY IS LOVINGLY
AND HARMONIOUSLY
DRAWN TO ME"**

**"I DON'T NEED MONEY,
MONEY NEEDS ME. I
JUST ACCEPT IT AND
LOVE IT"**

**"I AM MONEY"**

**"I ALLOW MONEY TO
TO COME AND GO AS
IT PLEASES"**

**"I AM PATIENT
AND I AM POISE"**

**"I ACCEPT WHAT IS FOR
ME AND LET GO WHAT IS
NOT"**

# "I HAVE NO ATTATCHMENTS"

# "I AM RECEPTIVE OF MORE…"

# "I AM NOW RECEIVING…"

# "I AM SUCCESS"

# "LIFE IS EASY"

# "I AM STRONG- MENTALLY, PHYSICALLY, SPIRITUALLY, AND EMOTIONALLY."

# "I AM HEALTHY- MENTALLY, PHYSICALLY, SPIRITUALLY, MOTIONALLY, AND FINANCIALLY"

# "I AM WEALTHY"

# "I AM RICH- MENTALLY, PHYSICALLY, SPIRITUALLY, EMOTIONALLY, AND FINANCIALLY"

**"I AM CONSTANTLY PROGRESSING"**

**"I RELEASE A NEED TO CONTROL"**

**"I HAVE AN ABUNDANCE OF ALL"**

**"I AM CONFIDENT"**

**"I AM COURAGEOUS"**

**"I AM INTELLIGENT"**

**"I AM FEARLESS"**

**"I AM DOUBTLESS"**

**"I AM AN INTELLECTUAL"**

**"I AM PEACE"**

**"I AM A PROTECTOR"**

**"I AM A PROVIDER"**

**"I AM HONEST"**

**"I AM GENUINE"**

**"I AM AUTHENTIC"**

**"I AM RESPONSIBLE"**

**"I AM RESPECTFUL"**

**"I AM SUCCESSFUL AND WILL
CONTINUE TO REACH HIGHER
LEVELS OF SUCCESS"**

**"I AM GREATNESS AND WILL
CONTINUE TO REACH HIGHER
LEVELS OF GREATNESS"**

**"I AM HAPPY"**

**"I AM OPTIMISTIC"**

**"I AM FILLED WITH GREAT
VIBES"**

**"I ONLY GENERATE AND ATTRACT POSITIVITY, LOVE, AND GREAT VIBES"**

**"I AM AN ATTRACTION FOR SUCCESS"**

**"I AM AN ATTRACTION FOR LOVE"**

**"I AM AMBITIOUS"**

**"I AM HARDWORKING."**

**"I AM SKILLFUL"**

**"I AM TALENTED"**

**"I AM GRITTY."**

**"I AM PROGRESSIVE"**

**"I AM LEGENDARY"**

**"I AM KNOWLEDGEABLE"**

**"I AM WISE"**

**"I AM A TEACHER WHO
CONTINUES TO SPREAD
KNOWLEDGE"**

**"I AM A STUDENT WHO
CONTINUES TO RECEIVE
KNOWLEDGE"**

**"I AM A MASTER FOLLOWER"**

**"I AM A MASTER LEADER"**

**"I AM MASTER STUDENT"**

**"I AM MASTER TEACHER"**

**"I AM A MASTER-MANIFESTER"**

**"I AM REAWRDED WITH
GREATER FINANCIAL
ABUNDANCE"**

**"I AM A MASTER OF SELF"**

**"I AM POWERFUL"**

**"I AM ONE WITH MY HIGHER-SELF. MY HIGHER-SELF CONTINUES TO GUIDE ME."**

**"I WILL CONTINUE TO ACCEPT AND FOLLOW THE SIGNS PRESENTED TO ME"**

**"MY SUBCONSCIOUS CONTINUES TO HEAL ME"**

**"I AM A CREATOR"**

**"I AM GOD, AND I WILL CONTINUE TO USE MY GOD ABILITIES TO CREATE THE LIFE I DESIRE"**

**"I AM A MILLIONAIRE"**

**"SUCCESS IS INEVITABLE"**

**"I REFLECT NOTHING BUT LOVE"**

# "I AM A SUCCESSFUL ENTREPRENEUR"

# "I AM A SUCCESSFUL BESTSELLING AUTHOR"

# "I AM A SUCCESSFUL PUBLIC SPEAKER"

# "I AM ONE WITH MY HIGHERSELF"

# "I AM IN SYNCHRONICTYAND ALIGNEMENT WITH MY GREATEST DESIRES"

# "I AM IN SYNCHRONICTYAND ALIGNEMENT WITH MY GREATER PURPOSE"

# "IT IS ALREADY HERE"

# "I AM AN ABUNDACE OF LIFE"

# "I AM FINANCIALLY ABUNDANT"

**"EVERYHTING IS CONPSIRING IN MY FAVOR"**

**"I AM BEAUTIFUL"**

**"EVERYDAY IN EVERYWAY MY WEALTH IS INCREASING"**

**"I AM WEALTH"**

**"I AM RICHES"**

**"I AM POWERFUL"**

**"I AM A MASTER STUDENT WHO CONTINUES TO RECEIVE KNOLWEDGE"**

**"I AM EFFICENT IN EVERY MANNER OF MY LIFE"**

**"I AM A MASTER TEACHER WHO CONTINUES TO SPREAD KNOWLEDGE"**

**"LIFE IS LOVE, LOVE IS LIFE"**

**"I AM PRONOIA"**

**"I AM AN ALCHEMIST"**

**"I AM LIMITLESS"**

**"I AM THAT I AM"**

**"ALL IS ONE"**

**"I AM CHARASMATIC, HANDSOME AND AN ATTRACTION FOR LOVE"**

**"ALL IS A REFLECTION OF I AM"**

**"I AM A CHEERFUL GIVER"**

**"I LOVE MY..."**

**"I MANIFEST MIRACLES"**

**"IT'S ALREADY DONE"**

**"MY LIFE IS FILLED WITH BLESSINGS"**

**"ALL IS CONSPIRING IN MY FAVOR"**

**"I SUBMIT TO MY HIGHER SELF"**
**"IT'S OK TO BE ANGRY, SAD, ALONE"**

**"MY HIGHS ALWAYS OUTWAY MY LOWS"**

**"I AM SURROUNDED BY PROSPERITY"**

**"I HAVE ALL THAT I NEED"**

**"I GIVE ALL CONTROL TO MY HIGHER SELF"**

**"I CONTINUE TO CREATE THE LIFE I DESIRE"**

**"I AM LIVING MY DESIRES"**

# "I USE MY MANIFEST AS ASSETS"

# "I RELEASE ANY PAIN, FEAR, WORRIES AND DOUBT"

# "I RELEASE AND REMOVE ANY SICKNESS OR ILLNESS FROM MY BODY"

# "I SEE AND CONSTRUCT PROSPERITY LOVINGLY AND HARMONIOUSLY"

# "I HAVE AN ABUNDANCE TO SHARE AND ABUNDANCE TO SPARE"

# "I AM INTENTIONAL IN MY ACTIONS"

# "MY INTENTIONS ARE PURE"

# "I RECEIVE AND IN EXCHANGE I GIVE TO THE UNIVERSE…"
# "I ONLY VIBRATE HIGHER"

"EVERYDAY I AM A BETTER VERSION OF MYSELF"

"I AM COMPLETE"

"I WAS DESTINED FOR FINANCIAL FREEDOM"

"I GIVE MY TALENTS AND SKILLSETS TO THE UNIVERSE IN ECHANGE FOR FINANCES"

"MY MIND IS DISCIPLINE ENOUGH THAT I ACCOMPLISH ANYTHING"

"I AM DESERVING OF WHAT THE UNIVERSE BRINGS ME"

"I LIVE IN THE PRESENT NEVER DWELLING ON THE PAST NEVER WORRIED ABOUT THE FUTURE"

"RICHES FLOW TO ME"

**"IF I VISUALIZE IT IT'S REAL
I MANIFEST IT INTO THE
PHYSICAL"**

**"I AM WALKING IN MY PURPOSE"**
**"MY IMAGINATION IS MY
REALITY"**

**"I ACCEPT... LOVING AND
HARMONIOUSLY"**

**"I SERVE FOR GREATER GOOD"**

**"I DON'T HAVE TO BELIEVE.
I KNOW"**

**"I AM A HIGHLY EVOLVED
BEING"**

**"EVERYDAY I WAKE UP
TO AND ATTRACT MORE
BLESSINGS"**

**"I AM DIVINE"**

Shelby Parris

# JOURNAL

Shelby Parris

**DATE:**

**INTENT:**

_____

_____

_____

_____

_____

**I AM:**

_____

_____

_____

_____

_____

**I AM GRATEFUL FOR:**

_____

_____

_____

_____

_____

**DATE:**

**INTENT:**

_____

_____

_____

_____

_____

**I AM:**

_____

_____

_____

_____

_____

**I AM GRATEFUL FOR:**

_____

_____

_____

_____

_____

**DATE:**

**INTENT:**

_____

_____

_____

_____

_____

**I AM:**

_____

_____

_____

_____

_____

**I AM GRATEFUL FOR:**

_____

_____

_____

_____

_____

**DATE:**

**INTENT:**

_____

_____

_____

_____

_____

**I AM:**

_____

_____

_____

_____

_____

**I AM GRATEFUL FOR:**

_____

_____

_____

_____

_____

Change Your Subconscious and Accomplish:
Manifesting Affirmations

**DATE:**

**INTENT:**

_____

_____

_____

_____

_____

_____

**I AM:**

_____

_____

_____

_____

_____

**I AM GRATEFUL FOR:**

_____

_____

_____

_____

_____

**DATE:**

**INTENT:**

_____

_____

_____

_____

_____

**I AM:**

_____

_____

_____

_____

_____

**I AM GRATEFUL FOR:**

_____

_____

_____

_____

_____

**DATE:**

**INTENT:**

_____

_____

_____

_____

_____

**I AM:**

_____

_____

_____

_____

_____

**I AM GRATEFUL FOR:**

_____

_____

_____

_____

_____

**DATE:**

**INTENT:**

_____
_____
_____
_____
_____

**I AM:**

_____
_____
_____
_____
_____

**I AM GRATEFUL FOR:**

_____
_____
_____
_____
_____

**DATE:**

**INTENT:**

_____

_____

_____

_____

_____

**I AM:**

_____

_____

_____

_____

_____

**I AM GRATEFUL FOR:**

_____

_____

_____

_____

_____

**DATE:**

**INTENT:**

_____

_____

_____

_____

_____

**I AM:**

_____

_____

_____

_____

_____

**I AM GRATEFUL FOR:**

_____

_____

_____

_____

_____

**DATE:**

**INTENT:**

_____

_____

_____

_____

_____

_____

**I AM:**

_____

_____

_____

_____

_____

**I AM GRATEFUL FOR:**

_____

_____

_____

_____

_____

**DATE:**

**INTENT...**

_____
_____
_____
_____
_____
_____

**I AM:**

_____
_____
_____
_____
_____

**I AM GRATEFUL FOR:**

_____
_____
_____
_____
_____

**DATE:**

**INTENT:**

_____

_____

_____

_____

_____

**I AM:**

_____

_____

_____

_____

_____

**I AM GRATEFUL FOR:**

_____

_____

_____

_____

_____

**DATE:**

**INTENT:**

_____

_____

_____

_____

_____

_____

**I AM:**

_____

_____

_____

_____

_____

**I AM GRATEFUL FOR:**

_____

_____

_____

_____

_____

**DATE:**

**INTENT:**

_____

_____

_____

_____

_____

_____

**I AM:**

_____

_____

_____

_____

_____

**I AM GRATEFUL FOR:**

_____

_____

_____

_____

_____

**DATE:**

**INTENT:**

_____

_____

_____

_____

_____

**I AM:**

_____

_____

_____

_____

_____

**I AM GRATEFUL FOR:**

_____

_____

_____

_____

_____

**DATE:**

**INTENT:**

_____

_____

_____

_____

_____

**I AM:**

_____

_____

_____

_____

_____

**I AM GRATEFUL FOR:**

_____

_____

_____

_____

_____

**DATE:**

**INTENT:**

_____

_____

_____

_____

_____

**I AM:**

_____

_____

_____

_____

_____

**I AM GRATEFUL FOR:**

_____

_____

_____

_____

_____

**DATE:**

**INTENT:**

_____

_____

_____

_____

_____

**I AM:**

_____

_____

_____

_____

_____

**I AM GRATEFUL FOR:**

_____

_____

_____

_____

_____

**DATE:**

**INTENT:**

_____

_____

_____

_____

_____

**I AM:**

_____

_____

_____

_____

_____

**I AM GRATEFUL FOR:**

_____

_____

_____

_____

_____

**DATE:**

**INTENT:**

_____

_____

_____

_____

_____

**I AM:**

_____

_____

_____

_____

_____

**I AM GRATEFUL FOR:**

_____

_____

_____

_____

_____

**DATE:**

**INTENT:**

_____

_____

_____

_____

_____

**I AM:**

_____

_____

_____

_____

_____

**I AM GRATEFUL FOR:**

_____

_____

_____

_____

_____

**DATE:**

**INTENT:**

_____

_____

_____

_____

_____

**I AM:**

_____

_____

_____

_____

_____

**I AM GRATEFUL FOR:**

_____

_____

_____

_____

_____

**DATE:**

**INTENT:**

_____

_____

_____

_____

_____

**I AM:**

_____

_____

_____

_____

_____

**I AM GRATEFUL FOR:**

_____

_____

_____

_____

_____

**DATE:**

**INTENT:**

_____

_____

_____

_____

_____

**I AM:**

_____

_____

_____

_____

_____

**I AM GRATEFUL FOR:**

_____

_____

_____

_____

_____

**DATE:**

**INTENT:**

_____

_____

_____

_____

_____

**I AM:**

_____

_____

_____

_____

_____

**I AM GRATEFUL FOR:**

_____

_____

_____

_____

_____

**DATE:**

**INTENT:**

_____

_____

_____

_____

_____

**I AM:**

_____

_____

_____

_____

_____

**I AM GRATEFUL FOR:**

_____

_____

_____

_____

_____

**DATE:**

**INTENT:**

_____

_____

_____

_____

_____

**I AM:**

_____

_____

_____

_____

_____

**I AM GRATEFUL FOR:**

_____

_____

_____

_____

_____

**DATE:**

**INTENT:**

_____

_____

_____

_____

_____

_____

**I AM:**

_____

_____

_____

_____

_____

**I AM GRATEFUL FOR:**

_____

_____

_____

_____

_____

**DATE:**

**INTENT:**

_____

_____

_____

_____

_____

**I AM:**

_____

_____

_____

_____

_____

**I AM GRATEFUL FOR:**

_____

_____

_____

_____

_____

Change Your Subconscious and Accomplish:
Manifesting Affirmations

**DATE:**

**INTENT:**

_____

_____

_____

_____

_____

**I AM:**

_____

_____

_____

_____

_____

**I AM GRATEFUL FOR:**

_____

_____

_____

_____

_____

**DATE:**

**INTENT:**

_____

_____

_____

_____

_____

**I AM:**

_____

_____

_____

_____

_____

**I AM GRATEFUL FOR:**

_____

_____

_____

_____

_____

**DATE:**

**INTENT:**

_____

_____

_____

_____

_____

**I AM:**

_____

_____

_____

_____

_____

**I AM GRATEFUL FOR:**

_____

_____

_____

_____

_____

**DATE:**

**INTENT:**

_____
_____
_____
_____
_____
_____

**I AM:**

_____
_____
_____
_____
_____

**I AM GRATEFUL FOR:**

_____
_____
_____
_____
_____
_____

Change Your Subconscious and Accomplish:
Manifesting Affirmations

**DATE:**

**INTENT:**

_____

_____

_____

_____

_____

**I AM:**

_____

_____

_____

_____

_____

**I AM GRATEFUL FOR:**

_____

_____

_____

_____

_____

**DATE:**

**INTENT:**

_____

_____

_____

_____

_____

**I AM:**

_____

_____

_____

_____

_____

**I AM GRATEFUL FOR:**

_____

_____

_____

_____

_____

**DATE:**

**INTENT:**

_____

_____

_____

_____

_____

**I AM:**

_____

_____

_____

_____

_____

**I AM GRATEFUL FOR:**

_____

_____

_____

_____

_____

**DATE:**

**INTENT:**

_____

_____

_____

_____

_____

**I AM:**

_____

_____

_____

_____

_____

**I AM GRATEFUL FOR:**

_____

_____

_____

_____

_____

**DATE:**

**INTENT:**

_____

_____

_____

_____

_____

_____

**I AM:**

_____

_____

_____

_____

_____

**I AM GRATEFUL FOR:**

_____

_____

_____

_____

_____

**DATE:**

**INTENT:**

_____

_____

_____

_____

_____

**I AM:**

_____

_____

_____

_____

_____

**I AM GRATEFUL FOR:**

_____

_____

_____

_____

_____

**DATE:**

**INTENT:**

_____

_____

_____

_____

_____

**I AM:**

_____

_____

_____

_____

_____

**I AM GRATEFUL FOR:**

_____

_____

_____

_____

_____

**DATE:**

**INTENT:**

_____

_____

_____

_____

_____

**I AM:**

_____

_____

_____

_____

_____

**I AM GRATEFUL FOR:**

_____

_____

_____

_____

_____

**DATE:**

**INTENT:**

_____

_____

_____

_____

_____

**I AM:**

_____

_____

_____

_____

_____

**I AM GRATEFUL FOR:**

_____

_____

_____

_____

_____

**DATE:**

**INTENT:**

_____

_____

_____

_____

_____

**I AM:**

_____

_____

_____

_____

_____

**I AM GRATEFUL FOR:**

_____

_____

_____

_____

_____

Change Your Subconscious and Accomplish:
Manifesting Affirmations

**DATE:**

**INTENT:**

_____

_____

_____

_____

_____

_____

**I AM:**

_____

_____

_____

_____

_____

**I AM GRATEFUL FOR:**

_____

_____

_____

_____

_____

**DATE:**

**INTENT:**

_____

_____

_____

_____

_____

_____

**I AM:**

_____

_____

_____

_____

_____

**I AM GRATEFUL FOR:**

_____

_____

_____

_____

_____

**DATE:**

**INTENT:**

_____

_____

_____

_____

_____

**I AM:**

_____

_____

_____

_____

_____

**I AM GRATEFUL FOR:**

_____

_____

_____

_____

_____

**DATE:**

**INTENT:**

_____

_____

_____

_____

_____

**I AM:**

_____

_____

_____

_____

_____

**I AM GRATEFUL FOR:**

_____

_____

_____

_____

_____

**DATE:**

**INTENT:**

_____

_____

_____

_____

_____

**I AM:**

_____

_____

_____

_____

_____

**I AM GRATEFUL FOR:**

_____

_____

_____

_____

_____

**DATE:**

**INTENT:**

_____

_____

_____

_____

_____

**I AM:**

_____

_____

_____

_____

_____

**I AM GRATEFUL FOR:**

_____

_____

_____

_____

_____

**DATE:**

**INTENT:**

_____

_____

_____

_____

_____

_____

**I AM:**

_____

_____

_____

_____

_____

**I AM GRATEFUL FOR:**

_____

_____

_____

_____

_____

**DATE:**

**INTENT:**

_____

_____

_____

_____

_____

**I AM:**

_____

_____

_____

_____

_____

**I AM GRATEFUL FOR:**

_____

_____

_____

_____

_____

**DATE:**

**INTENT:**

_____

_____

_____

_____

_____

**I AM:**

_____

_____

_____

_____

_____

**I AM GRATEFUL FOR:**

_____

_____

_____

_____

_____

**DATE:**

**INTENT:**

_____

_____

_____

_____

_____

**I AM:**

_____

_____

_____

_____

_____

**I AM GRATEFUL FOR:**

_____

_____

_____

_____

_____

**DATE:**

**INTENT:**

_____

_____

_____

_____

_____

_____

**I AM:**

_____

_____

_____

_____

_____

**I AM GRATEFUL FOR:**

_____

_____

_____

_____

_____

**DATE:**

**INTENT:**

_____

_____

_____

_____

_____

**I AM:**

_____

_____

_____

_____

_____

**I AM GRATEFUL FOR:**

_____

_____

_____

_____

_____

**DATE:**

**INTENT:**

_____

_____

_____

_____

_____

**I AM:**

_____

_____

_____

_____

_____

**I AM GRATEFUL FOR:**

_____

_____

_____

_____

_____

**DATE:**

**INTENT:**

_____

_____

_____

_____

_____

_____

**I AM:**

_____

_____

_____

_____

_____

**I AM GRATEFUL FOR:**

_____

_____

_____

_____

_____

_____

**DATE:**

**INTENT:**

_____

_____

_____

_____

_____

_____

**I AM:**

_____

_____

_____

_____

_____

**I AM GRATEFUL FOR:**

_____

_____

_____

_____

_____

**DATE:**

**INTENT:**

_____

_____

_____

_____

_____

_____

**I AM:**

_____

_____

_____

_____

_____

**I AM GRATEFUL FOR:**

_____

_____

_____

_____

_____

**DATE:**

**INTENT:**

_____

_____

_____

_____

_____

_____

**I AM:**

_____

_____

_____

_____

_____

**I AM GRATEFUL FOR:**

_____

_____

_____

_____

_____

**DATE:**

**INTENT:**

_____
_____
_____
_____
_____
_____

**I AM:**

_____
_____
_____
_____
_____

**I AM GRATEFUL FOR:**

_____
_____
_____
_____
_____

**DATE:**

**INTENT:**

_____

_____

_____

_____

_____

_____

**I AM:**

_____

_____

_____

_____

_____

**I AM GRATEFUL FOR:**

_____

_____

_____

_____

_____

**DATE:**

**INTENT:**

_____

_____

_____

_____

_____

**I AM:**

_____

_____

_____

_____

_____

**I AM GRATEFUL FOR:**

_____

_____

_____

_____

_____

**DATE:**

**INTENT:**

_____

_____

_____

_____

_____

**I AM:**

_____

_____

_____

_____

_____

**I AM GRATEFUL FOR:**

_____

_____

_____

_____

_____

**DATE:**

**INTENT:**

_____
_____
_____
_____
_____
_____

**I AM:**

_____
_____
_____
_____
_____

**I AM GRATEFUL FOR:**

_____
_____
_____
_____
_____

**DATE:**

**INTENT:**

_____

_____

_____

_____

_____

**I AM:**

_____

_____

_____

_____

_____

**I AM GRATEFUL FOR:**

_____

_____

_____

_____

_____

**DATE:**

**INTENT:**

_____
_____
_____
_____
_____
_____

**I AM:**

_____
_____
_____
_____
_____

**I AM GRATEFUL FOR:**

_____
_____
_____
_____
_____

**DATE:**

**INTENT:**

_____

_____

_____

_____

_____

_____

**I AM:**

_____

_____

_____

_____

_____

**I AM GRATEFUL FOR:**

_____

_____

_____

_____

_____

**DATE:**

**INTENT:**

_____

_____

_____

_____

_____

_____

**I AM:**

_____

_____

_____

_____

_____

**I AM GRATEFUL FOR:**

_____

_____

_____

_____

_____

_____

**DATE:**

**INTENT:**

_____

_____

_____

_____

_____

_____

**I AM:**

_____

_____

_____

_____

_____

**I AM GRATEFUL FOR:**

_____

_____

_____

_____

_____

**DATE:**

**INTENT:**

_____

_____

_____

_____

_____

**I AM:**

_____

_____

_____

_____

_____

**I AM GRATEFUL FOR:**

_____

_____

_____

_____

_____

**DATE:**

**INTENT:**

_____

_____

_____

_____

_____


**I AM:**

_____

_____

_____

_____

_____


**I AM GRATEFUL FOR:**

_____

_____

_____

_____

_____

**DATE:**

**INTENT:**

_____

_____

_____

_____

_____

**I AM:**

_____

_____

_____

_____

_____

**I AM GRATEFUL FOR:**

_____

_____

_____

_____

_____

**DATE:**

**INTENT:**

_____

_____

_____

_____

_____

**I AM:**

_____

_____

_____

_____

_____

**I AM GRATEFUL FOR:**

_____

_____

_____

_____

_____

**DATE:**

**INTENT:**

_____
_____
_____
_____
_____
_____

**I AM:**

_____
_____
_____
_____
_____

**I AM GRATEFUL FOR:**

_____
_____
_____
_____
_____

**DATE:**

**INTENT:**

_____

_____

_____

_____

_____

**I AM:**

_____

_____

_____

_____

_____

**I AM GRATEFUL FOR:**

_____

_____

_____

_____

_____

**DATE:**

**INTENT:**

_____

_____

_____

_____

_____

**I AM:**

_____

_____

_____

_____

_____

**I AM GRATEFUL FOR:**

_____

_____

_____

_____

_____

**DATE:**

**INTENT:**

_____

_____

_____

_____

_____

**I AM:**

_____

_____

_____

_____

_____

**I AM GRATEFUL FOR:**

_____

_____

_____

_____

_____

**DATE:**

**INTENT:**

_____

_____

_____

_____

_____

**I AM:**

_____

_____

_____

_____

_____

**I AM GRATEFUL FOR:**

_____

_____

_____

_____

_____

**DATE:**

**INTENT:**

_____

_____

_____

_____

_____

_____

**I AM:**

_____

_____

_____

_____

_____

**I AM GRATEFUL FOR:**

_____

_____

_____

_____

_____

**DATE:**

**INTENT:**

_____
_____
_____
_____
_____
_____

**I AM:**

_____
_____
_____
_____
_____

**I AM GRATEFUL FOR:**

_____
_____
_____
_____
_____
_____

**DATE:**

**INTENT:**

_____

_____

_____

_____

_____

_____

**I AM:**

_____

_____

_____

_____

_____

**I AM GRATEFUL FOR:**

_____

_____

_____

_____

_____

**DATE:**

**INTENT:**

_____

_____

_____

_____

_____

_____

**I AM:**

_____

_____

_____

_____

_____

**I AM GRATEFUL FOR:**

_____

_____

_____

_____

_____

**DATE:**

**INTENT:**

_____

_____

_____

_____

_____

**I AM:**

_____

_____

_____

_____

_____

**I AM GRATEFUL FOR:**

_____

_____

_____

_____

_____

**DATE:**

**INTENT:**

_____

_____

_____

_____

_____

_____

**I AM:**

_____

_____

_____

_____

_____

**I AM GRATEFUL FOR:**

_____

_____

_____

_____

_____

Change Your Subconscious and Accomplish:
Manifesting Affirmations

**DATE:**

**INTENT:**

_____

_____

_____

_____

_____

**I AM:**

_____

_____

_____

_____

_____

**I AM GRATEFUL FOR:**

_____

_____

_____

_____

_____

**DATE:**

**INTENT:**

_____

_____

_____

_____

_____

_____

**I AM:**

_____

_____

_____

_____

_____

**I AM GRATEFUL FOR:**

_____

_____

_____

_____

_____

_____

**DATE:**

**INTENT:**

_____

_____

_____

_____

_____

**I AM:**

_____

_____

_____

_____

_____

**I AM GRATEFUL FOR:**

_____

_____

_____

_____

_____

**DATE:**

**INTENT:**

_____

_____

_____

_____

_____

**I AM:**

_____

_____

_____

_____

_____

**I AM GRATEFUL FOR:**

_____

_____

_____

_____

_____

**DATE:**

**INTENT:**

_____

_____

_____

_____

_____


**I AM:**

_____

_____

_____

_____

_____


**I AM GRATEFUL FOR:**

_____

_____

_____

_____

_____

**DATE:**

**INTENT:**

_____

_____

_____

_____

_____

**I AM:**

_____

_____

_____

_____

_____

**I AM GRATEFUL FOR:**

_____

_____

_____

_____

_____

**DATE:**

**INTENT:**

_____

_____

_____

_____

_____

_____

**I AM:**

_____

_____

_____

_____

_____

**I AM GRATEFUL FOR:**

_____

_____

_____

_____

_____

**DATE:**

**INTENT:**

_____

_____

_____

_____

_____

**I AM:**

_____

_____

_____

_____

_____

**I AM GRATEFUL FOR:**

_____

_____

_____

_____

_____

**DATE:**

**INTENT:**

_____

_____

_____

_____

_____

_____

**I AM:**

_____

_____

_____

_____

_____

**I AM GRATEFUL FOR:**

_____

_____

_____

_____

_____

**DATE:**

**INTENT:**

_____

_____

_____

_____

_____

**I AM:**

_____

_____

_____

_____

_____

**I AM GRATEFUL FOR:**

_____

_____

_____

_____

_____

**DATE:**

**INTENT:**

_____

_____

_____

_____

_____

**I AM:**

_____

_____

_____

_____

_____

**I AM GRATEFUL FOR:**

_____

_____

_____

_____

_____

Made in the USA
Coppell, TX
01 June 2020

26810368R00075